Born to be Wild
Little Sheep

Christian Marie

Words that appear in the glossary are printed in
boldface type the first time they occur in the text.

GARETH**STEVENS**
GS
PUBLISHING
A Member of the WHC Media Family of Companies

Welcome to Life

A newborn sheep, which is called a lamb, looks weak and wobbly. It has shaky legs; a small, triangular-shaped head; big ears; a thin tail; and a fuzzy coat. When it is born, a little lamb is wet all over. Its mother, called a ewe (sounds like "you"), licks the lamb's coat thoroughly. Most lambs weigh between 6 and 10 pounds (3 and 5 kilograms) at birth — the same weight as most human babies. Unlike human babies, however, little lambs do not wait ten or twelve months to start walking. About thirty minutes after it is born, a lamb can already stand and take its first steps.

The first time a newborn lamb tries to stand it may fall down, because its thin legs are too shaky to hold it. When it tries again, however, the lamb is usually able to take a few steps.

What do you think?

Why does a ewe lick her lamb after it is born?

a) to dry the lamb's coat and keep the lamb warm

b) to make the lamb's coat look pretty

c) to teach the lamb how to stay clean

A ewe licks her lamb after it is born to dry its coat and keep the lamb warm.

A female sheep carries an unborn lamb inside her body for about five months. When she is ready to give birth, she seems to become nervous or fussy. Scratching the ground with her hoof, the ewe bleats, or cries, and looks for a quiet place to have her baby. When a lamb is born, its front legs usually come out first, followed by its head and then the rest of its body. A newborn lamb is all wet, and its mother quickly begins licking it to dry its coat so the lamb will stay warm.

A lamb does not always arrive alone. Sometimes, a ewe gives birth to two or three lambs at a time.

After a lamb is born, we say the ewe "has lambed." When a ewe has more than one lamb at a time, the babies are usually born about fifteen minutes apart.

Little sheep are called lambs until they are one year old. Some kinds of sheep are raised for their wool. Others are raised for their meat. Still other kinds of sheep are raised for their rich milk, which is made into cheese and other dairy foods.

Adult male sheep are called rams. Some rams have horns, depending on their **breed**. In breeds that have horned rams, the ewes may also have horns or the stumps of horns.

Eating Can Be Hard Work

A little lamb's first food is its mother's milk. Lambs drink their mothers' milk for about three months. To drink from its mother's body, a young lamb has to kneel down on its front legs, spread its back legs for balance, and tuck its head underneath its mother's stomach. In this position, it can grab one of the **teats** that stick out from its mother's **udder** and begin to drink. To make the milk come out faster, the lamb will bump its head against the teat. A little lamb usually wags its tail while it is drinking, too.

What do you think ?

What do lambs eat when they stop drinking milk?

a) fruits and vegetables

b) meat and fish

c) grass and other plants

The milk that a lamb drinks during the first few days after it is born contains rich **nutrients** that protect the lamb against diseases. Milk is a lamb's main food until it is about three months old.

When lambs stop drinking milk, they eat grass and other plants.

Older lambs and adult sheep are herbivores, which means they eat only grass and other plants. Sheep are also **ruminant mammals**, which means their stomachs have four parts. When it eats, a sheep bites off grass with its front teeth and grinds the grass into balls with its back teeth. When it swallows the balls of grass, they go into one part of its stomach. Later, while the sheep is resting, it brings the grass back up into its mouth and chews it for a long time before swallowing it again. This time, the grass is broken down and absorbed by the other parts of the sheep's stomach.

When it is about three weeks old, a lamb copies its mother and begins to eat grass.

Sheep get some of the water they need from their food, but they still have to drink fresh water, too.

During winter, sheep live in a shelter or pen called a sheepfold. The sheep farmer or **shepherd** feeds them hay; grains, such as wheat, barley, oats, or rye; and cattle cake, which is a block of food made of sunflower or soybean seeds.

No Wool Without Sheep

Many sheep are white, but sheep can also be black, brown, or beige. Some have short, curly wool, others have long, silky wool — or short, silky wool or long, curly wool! Not every sheep, however, has a wool coat. Some have coarse hair instead. Some sheep are tall and strong, others are small but may be more **agile**. In telling one breed of sheep from another, size or weight is not as important as the animals' other features.

These sheep have short, tight, white wool covering their bodies. They belong to a breed of large sheep that is very common in the western United States.

What do you think?

How many different breeds of sheep are there in the world?

a) about eighteen

b) about eighty

c) about eight hundred

About eight hundred different breeds of sheep can be found around the world.

Some people might think that all sheep are alike, but there are about eight hundred different breeds of sheep throughout the world. Some breeds live on grassy plains, while others live on high, windy plateaus where grass is difficult to grow. Some kinds of sheep live in places where the Sun is hot, others live in cool seaside meadows. Breeds of sheep look different from one another because, over time, their bodies have **adapted** to the climates of the places where they live.

A Jacob sheep can have as many as six horns on its head. Its wool coat is white with black spots.

A Lacaune sheep has floppy ears but no horns. It is a tall sheep and does not have any wool on its stomach or its legs. The Lacaune ewe's milk is used to produce Roquefort cheese, which is known for its strong, sharp smell.

Castilian rams have long horns that grow to form big loops. These sheep live in the Pyrenees mountains in Spain and France and have adapted to the fog, moisture, and snow of the mountains.

A Suffolk sheep has a fuzzy white coat, except on its head and the bottoms of its legs, which are covered with smooth, black hair. A Suffolk sheep also has long, thin, floppy ears.

Sticking Close Together

When a little lamb is napping quietly in the grass next to its mother, its eyes are closed or partly shut. Its back legs are folded under its body, and its front legs are tucked under its chest. But don't be fooled! Although the young lamb might look relaxed, it is always on guard.

Lambs and sheep are always afraid, and anything can startle them — a strange noise, the arrival of another kind of animal, or trouble among the sheep. As soon as sleeping lambs sense that something is wrong, they stand up and are ready to run.

What do you think?

Why do sheep always stay close together?

a) because they want to keep warm

b) because they like each other a lot

c) because they want to be safe

Just like adult sheep, lambs do not sleep long or very soundly. They are always watching and listening for danger.

Sheep always stay close together because they want to be safe.

Most sheep have no way to defend themselves. In case of danger, the only thing they can do is run away. Sheep live together in a group called a **flock**. When the flock is safe inside a fenced meadow, the sheep separate and scatter to graze on, or eat, grass and other plants. A sheep always makes sure, however, that it can see the rest of the flock and that the other sheep are not too far away. If one sheep moves very far, all the others follow it, and then they all stand very close together. When they are traveling, all the sheep in a flock try to stay as close to each other as possible.

Because lambs are smaller and slower than their mothers, they are in greater danger of being attacked by **predators**, such as coyotes. When lambs are afraid, they cry, or bleat.

When sheep travel, they form a tight group. One sheep, however, always takes the lead and walks ahead of the flock.

When sheep sense danger or any changes in their surroundings, they gather together tightly. The lambs stay in the center, surrounded by the adults, who stand squeezed up against each other.

In Warm Weather

The woolly coat that covers a sheep's body is called fleece. During winter, when the air temperature is very cold, a sheep's fleece becomes thicker to keep the sheep warm. During spring, when the temperature warms up, the sheep molts, or sheds, its winter coat. Often, a sheep farmer or a shepherd removes the sheep's coat by shearing, or cutting, it off. The sheep will gradually grow new fleece to keep it warm the following winter.

If you touch a sheep's wool fleece, it will feel a little oily. Sheep's wool is coated with a natural wax that is produced by the sheep's body. This waxy coating protects the sheep against rain or snow and helps keep the sheep warm.

What do you think ??

What do some kinds of sheep do in summer?

a) They stay in pens.

b) They move to the seashore.

c) They move to the mountains.

In summer, some kinds of sheep move to the mountains.

By summer, sheep have eaten all of the grass in the area nearest their pens and must move to what are called summer pastures. In some areas, sheep go up into the mountains to find fresh grass to eat. The lambs that were born in spring are now bigger and stronger and are ready to follow the flock as it travels long distances to find food. Sheep graze in their summer pastures from late spring until early fall.

After a sheep is sheared, its wool is shipped to a factory where it is spun into yarn or woven into cloth. Wool yarn is used to make blankets, rugs, sweaters, hats, and other clothing. Wool cloth is used to make clothing and furniture coverings.

Strong hooves help sheep walk the long distances to their summer pastures. A sheep's hoof covers two toes and is split in the middle.

Sheep are mammals. Eight hundred different breeds of domesticated, or tamed, sheep can be found around the world. The countries with the greatest number of sheep include China, Australia, India, Iran, and New Zealand. The United States has forty-seven breeds. Four breeds of wild sheep, including the bighorn sheep of North America, live in mountainous areas. Wild sheep have large horns and coats of hair instead of wool. Sheep live up to twenty years. Adult males weigh 165 to 400 pounds (75 to 180 kg). Females weigh 100 to 225 pounds (45 to 100 kg).

Sheep are related to goats.

A sheep's head is shaped like a triangle — wide at the top and narrow at the mouth.

Most adult sheep have short tails. Sheep farmers often cut off, or dock, a lamb's long, thin tail before the lamb becomes an adult.

Sheep have excellent hearing and can move their ears in different directions to hear sounds.

Sheep have two large nostrils. They use their sense of smell to find fresh water and grass and to detect predators.

At the end of each leg, a sheep has two toes covered by a toenail that forms the sheep's hoof. Sheep's hooves are called cloven hooves because they are split into two parts. Other animals with cloven hooves include cattle, goats, pigs, and giraffes.

Depending on its breed, a sheep's body is covered with a coat of either thick wool or coarse hair. The coats of different breeds may also be different colors.

GLOSSARY

adapted — changed to fit a set of conditions or a certain situation

agile — able to move quickly and easily

breed — (n) a particular group of animals that all have the same physical features and abilities

flock — a group of animals, such as sheep or birds, that live, eat, and travel together

mammals — warm-blooded animals that have backbones, give birth to live babies, feed their young milk from the mother's body, and have skin that is covered with hair or fur

nutrients — the parts of foods that help people and other animals grow and develop

predators — animals that hunt and kill other animals for food

ruminant — an animal with four stomachs that chews and swallows grass and other tough plants more than once. The food is brought back into the animal's mouth after being partly digested, or broken down.

shepherd — a person who takes care of a flock of sheep

teats — the small, nipplelike parts that stick out on an animal's udder and through which milk is drawn

udder — the body part that hangs on the underside of some animals, such as cows and sheep, and produces milk

Please visit our web site at: www.garethstevens.com
For a free color catalog describing Gareth Stevens Publishing's list of high-quality books and multimedia programs, call 1-800-542-2595 (USA) or 1-800-387-3178 (Canada). Gareth Stevens Publishing's fax: (414) 332-3567.

Library of Congress Cataloging-in-Publication Data

Marie, Christian.
  [Agneau. English]
  Little Sheep / Christian Marie. — North American ed.
    p. cm. — (Born to be wild)
  ISBN 0-8368-6169-8 (lib. bdg.)
  1. Lambs—Juvenile literature. 2. Sheep—Juvenile literature.
I. Title. II. Series.
SF376.5.M3713   2006
636.3'07—dc22   2005053156

This North American edition first published in 2006 by
Gareth Stevens Publishing
A Member of the WRC Media Family of Companies
330 West Olive Street, Suite 100
Milwaukee, Wisconsin 53212 USA

First published in 2002 as *L'agneau* by Mango Jeunesse, an imprint of Editions Mango, Paris, France. Addtional end matter copyright © 2006 by Gareth Stevens, Inc.

Picture Credits (t=top, b=bottom, l=left, r=right)
Cogis: Lanceau 2, 5(both), 10, 13(b), 22-23(both); Labat 12(br), 13(t); Gissey 14; Alexis 17; Varin 20. Hoaqui/Jacana: J. F. Lanzarone 8; S. Danegger 15. Phone: C. Thiriet back cover, title page, 4(both), 9(b), 16(r), 16(l); P. Roger 18. Sunset: Holt Studios 6; G. Lacz cover, 7, 9(t); P. Schwartz 11; Maier 12(tl); Marge 21.

English translation: Muriel Castille
Gareth Stevens editor: Barbara Kiely Miller
Gareth Stevens art direction: Tammy West
Gareth Stevens designer: Jenni Gaylord

Printed in the United States of America

1 2 3 4 5 6 7 8 9 10 09 08 07 06